I0471043

How to Make an extra Dollar

Copyright 2013
by John Stilwell

Create Space Edition

Limited license for the book cover was
purchased through BigStockPhoto.com

Non Fiction Books:

100 Ways to Save a Dollar without Lowering Your Lifestyle
The Independent Author's handbook - Second Edition
The Stilwell Family Cookbook
Tech Watch: The Future is being Built Today

Science Fiction Books:

The Puppy of Doom and Other Stories
In the Image of Gods
Beyond the Galactic Core
Tank (CD and MP3)
Wasn't Tomorrow Wonderful

Blogs:

JohnStilwell.blogspot.com
StilwellFamilyCookbook.blogspot.com
Techwatch2.blogspot.com
SmartTaveller2.blogspot.com

With the modest success of my first money book, focused on spending more efficiently, I have wanted to do another. I wanted to write a book about how to increase one's income. This is a subject highly dependant on one's life situation and interests. How could such a book have any chance to be useful to every reader? I had to shrink the scope drastically. Then one day I was thinking about how we all used to make extra money as children. We would go outside to the sidewalk in front of our homes and sell lemonade. Or we'd ask mom for a chore and spend the next hour ironing shirts. What is the adult equivalent? The more I looked into it the more I found. I stopped counting when I reached fifty ideas. I have done many of the things in this book myself. The following are ideas, advice, tips, tools game plans and the occasional personal story.

Money is critically important to you as an adult. Protect the cash flow at all costs. But when it shrinks, you only have two options, spend less or make more. All of the following ideas are how to make extra money on the side short of changing careers or starting a full time business. They are presented like popcorn, small, easy to chew and lots of them. Not all may be appropriate for your circumstances. The running theme is to suggest ones that you can use to start generating income in six months or less. They stop short of starting a real business though most could be the first step in just such a direction. I'll also provide answers to questions such as, "Do you need a license?" and "What about income tax?"

Table of Contents

Introduction...6
Make an extra dollar at work 11
  Other duties than assigned...........................11
  Professional don't have the same opportunities...12
  Get a part-time job. 14
  Income Taxes..16
Resume and Job Interview Tips 17
  Information that must be easy to find.........17
  What will hurt you? 19
  Some things don't matter. 19
  What will help you? 20
  Interview Tips 21
14 Ways to become a favorite Employee........23
Turn your Home into Income 26
  **Most of the time, even a renter can have a
  renter.**..27
  Renting a room in your home as the owner.28
  Rent a room part-time. 30
  Finding renters. 32
  Background checks. 34
  Is your house or property near a stadium? 36
  Do you have extra storage space?................36
  Do you have something special like a pier? 37
Build a Real Estate Empire!............................38
  You can rent a vacation house part-time.....42
  What to do with an empty lot. 43
  What to do with empty land..........................44
  Income Taxes..45
Getting started buying stocks 49
Make Money from your Hobby 60

Why not collect gold, gems and money as a hobby? 60
Sell what you make 61
Planes and boats. 63
Water sports 64
Art and Photography 64
Raid your closet of unwanted stuff! 68
Make Money as an Author 70
Selling an article or short story the old fashioned way 71
Selling an article or a short story the new fashioned way 72
Beyond e-books 73
Make Money by making Movies! 78
Make extra money by providing a service 83
About the Author 100
Appendix A: Useful links 101

Introduction

When you are a child and need a couple of dollars, you either ask your mother for a chore or you set up a lemonade stand. The following is the adult equivalent. Although any one could turn into a new career, the intention is to make some extra money on the side. The assumption is that you are reasonably happy with your job and only want to make a little extra money. Maybe you would like your hobby to pay for itself. Perhaps you are between jobs and need to make some income while you wait for that great new opportunity to materialize.

Success is paying all of your own bills
while maintaining a life style
where you are happy
a reasonable amount of the time.

Your finances amount to a triangle. How much you make, how much you spend and how you invest the difference. This list of ideas is focused on how to increase the amount of money you make short of changing careers.

The ideas we will talk about fall into the category of part-time. Some require for you to be twenty one or older. Many are fine for an eighteen year old. They all stop short of starting a real business, no bank loans, accountants, papers of incorporation are needed. But some will require a license or certificate. If training is needed, it can be acquired in 6 months or less. A few of the ideas will require a couple hundred dollars up front depending on what you already own. Most have no cost, requiring only your time. The goal is to get you to that extra stream of income in as soon as six months.

All of the ideas are honest. None are get-rich schemes. This book is light on philosophy and heavy on ideas. They are presented like popcorn. They are small, easy to chew and lots of them.

Thoughts to keep in mind:

What is your goal? Is it to not lose your house? Or is it to make beer money? Some of the ideas may be no fun but they can quickly get you extra cash. Others are fun but the income is less certain.

Compare profit you can and will make to a minimal wage job. If your success is worse than minimal wage you are best to stop and try a different idea. I've seen too many people over the years loose everything following a dream long after it was obvious that it wasn't going to pan out.

No gamblers math allowed. Gamblers brag about their winnings but won't admit their losses. Profit is income minus all costs. An example of costs or overhead would be transportation and material costs and fees. What counts is how much money is in your pocket at the end of a given time period. After all of the overhead bills are paid. Divide this by the hours you spent working.

Be honest to yourself. Everything will be some variation of a business. I know somebody who raises chickens in their backyard and sells the eggs. His income is a hundred and fifty dollars a month.

The chicken feed is $300 a month. He is losing money every month. They have been for two years. That is a loss of about $3,600! If he sold the 79 chickens to a butcher he'd only get $150. Trying and failing is fine but be ready to cut your losses if you get in too deep.

I know another person who bought fish tanks off Ebay and tried to resell them at a profit. He ended up with a house full of fish tanks. An idea like this is fine to try but start small and stop if you not in the right place at the right time.

If you are looking for extra income because you are bored and want to meet people, how much you make may not be very important. Turning your hobby into a money maker may be a painless option. When determining profit, the cost of the business can be just the extra money being spent due to the intent to make a profit.

Only try to get paid for what you know or what you can do. There are ideas in this book about how to start with nothing. In some cases, you need the proper licenses such as a general contractor license. If you don't already have one, you certainly can pursue this path if you like, but the road to extra income may be longer than six months.

People are busy. Most are willing to pay for part-time help.

Dress the part. Don't look like a gangster. If they come to you, clean your house and yard. Look like you have your act together.

You only have so much time and energy to devote to making money. Unlike my book of ideas of how to spend more efficiently, only a couple of the ideas in this book can be used at the same time. Why? There are only so many hours in the day. Look at all of the options and pick the best for you. You may want to rotate between ideas based on the season or your personal situation.

Advertising: Letting them come to you is less threatening than you knocking on their door. Be able to provide references. When you have your salesman hat on, be careful not to oversell yourself. But be confident. Underselling can also be a bad thing.

Get rich quick schemes usually make somebody other than you rich. Unfortunately they can be hard to spot. Is buying a parking lot really what you want to get into? But if you already have a piece of land that could be used as a parking lot, well, this is the sort of idea we'll explore.

Risks

What if you get hurt or cause damage? If you don't have insurance you may want to get it.

If somebody is hiring part-time help and the pay is too good to be true, it is. Beware of crooks and

scammers. They especially target at-home workers.
You could find yourself in a far worse situation than
not getting paid. You could unwittingly become part
of a criminal venture and be left holding the bag when
the police show up.

Make an extra dollar at work

When you need to up your income the first reaction is that you need a raise or a new job. This is very reasonable to consider. Accomplishing it can be as simple as politely telling your boss that you need a raise. I have actually been in the position in my career where I was being skipped over for promotion because my boss didn't know I wanted a raise! Really? Really! He was serious. I had never complained about my pay so he only worried about promoting the others in the office.

<u>Other duties than assigned</u>

Never threaten to quit unless you really mean it. If your boss says no and you don't quit, you lose credibility. Worse yet, they can no longer count on you to be around when they need you so their focus will shift to another promising employee. Your plea for extra pay just made you minimized and unwanted.

Most likely your boss will say no. But you can counter with asking what can you do to get on the promotion list or work some extra hours. If you work at a restaurant or department store, you may be able to land an extra shift. Or, you can be on the top of your bosses call list for when other employees go on vacation or call in sick. Many employers pay extra for Sundays and holidays. If there is a third shift, are you willing to work through the night every night? People who work the graveyard shift get paid higher wages but their personal lives suffer. Working third shift temporarily can be a good option. Beware of frequently changing shifts. It will effect your sleeping and can often cause bouts of depression.

If your company is moving or the building is being renovated there may be opportunities for overtime. This is especially true if your office does sensitive, propriety or classified work. Even if you can't do the work yourself, there may be a need to watch the painters, plumbers, electricians and movers. If you owned a bank, would you let workers you had never met before run free and unsupervised after everybody went home for the day? Of course not.

Depending on where you work, you could get paid extra to be a professional witness. A classic example is to become a Notary Public. This can be a service you provide to the other employees if you are in a major corporation or government building. If you are in a small storefront of any kind, the store manager can advertise that you are a Notary Public and that there is an unexpected service available to customers. In this case, they'd likely want a piece of the action.

You can charge what you feel is reasonable. For the sake of discussion, how about $5 a page. You become a Notary Public by going to your local court house or post office and get a license, a Notary Stamp, log book and basic instruction. Expect this to cost in the ballpark of $125.

Professional don't have the same opportunities.

Professionals such as Doctors, lawyers, bankers, engineers don't typically work in shifts. For the corporate managers of the world, extra pay can be earned by going on a business trip or conference. The benefit is that for a week or more you are not incurring living expenses. You're meals and gas are paid for. There is likely a small daily stipend. The military and government call this per diem. It's extra money in your pocket to pay for a hotel, meals, transportation and miscellaneous expenses. If you are in an expensive city, this would be a higher amount. If you don't spend it, you usually get to keep it. The long the trip, the more this can add up. If your employer pays a flat rate, you may be allowed to stay in a cheaper hotel and eat at inexpensive restaurants and pocket the difference.

One trick to up the impact of a business trip is being able to take your family. My wife goes to conferences once or twice a year. Her work pays for her to fly there and her expenses during the conference. But if it is in a vacation spot, say Las Vegas why not stay several extra days? When she is not in the conference, we are on vacation and only had to pay for my plane ticket. Most employers don't care if there is a second occupant in the hotel room. At the worst you just have to pay the difference between the actual room cost and what the single occupancy charge would have been.

Another option for a corporate professional is committee work. This is typically hours of work above and beyond their normal duties. The task is to research and debate. As a group the committee produces a recommendation in writing. I've been on a lot of committees over the years. They increase your chances of getting promoted by making you look more ambitious than your piers. Sometimes committee members afterwards receive cash awards as a thank you for extra work. Neither is guaranteed. Frequently, committee members receive nothing regardless of what they are promised.

Consulting may be an option if the professional is an expert on the subject. The usual barrier is a non-competition clause in there contract. For an engineer with a professional certification or a college professor, this usually isn't an issue.

Whether you are a blue collar worker or a professional, one angle is to find a job with a business that provides entertainment such as a fishing boat, scuba, golf, white water rafting. Being a tour guide can be great way to find new friends. Often, employees and can use the services at a greatly reduced charge.

Major hotel chains like Hilton and Sheridan give their employees serious discounts on hotel rooms. Thus can save you money when you go on vacation. Airlines normally give their employees anywhere from discounted to free plane tickets. Usually you only have to pay the taxes.

What is your passion? Imagine getting paid to go white water rafting or scuba diving every weekend. You make a couple bucks and save a lot of money on free entertainment

Get a part-time job.

A second job is a straight forward and the least popular way to make an extra dollar. You need a stable schedule with your primary job to do this. If you have a job where you have to travel out of town or have a sickly family member at home to take care of, this may not be an option for you. If your second employer cannot count on you being available to work on their schedule, they won't want to hire you.

The classic part time job is at a hardware store, department store at Christmas or a Christmas tree lot. For many people, the job they did in high school is their fall back job when they need extra money. Jobs with tips often pay more. Pizza delivery, busboy, waiter, salesman and bartenders get paid a low hourly wage. But if you are likable, willing to work really hard and pick a employer who has a lot of customers, the tips alone could have you making more than your boss.

Your employer may have part-time jobs available. This can be very convenient and you avoid the annoying job interview process. Perhaps there is a need for temporary surge in warehouse workers. This could be a seasonal surge. Whether government or a contractor if you work in a secure facility, cleared people can be costly to hire. There may be after hour security or janitorial work available.

Most professionals have a harder time getting a part time job than blue collar workers. A software engineer who designs large computer systems for a living would naturally want to do the same on the weekend. But you can't do a big job like that for just a few hours a month. A medical professional such as a Nurse Practitioner is certified to give injections. There are plenty of businesses such as travel medicine that are happy to pay such a person a serious amount of money an hour to give vaccinations for a few hours a week.

Another problem professionals run into is the pay. Most part-time jobs pay minimum wage or slightly higher. For somebody who makes fifty dollars an hour and needs to increase their income, the prospect of making an extra twenty dollars for an afternoon of work just won't cut it. People like this often gravitate to other avenues such as starting a small business. They need work with flexible hours. I have seen this range from accounting to playing in a band.

Income Taxes

Depending on the type of work you do, you may be able to deduct some of your expenses on your taxes. Lower taxes means more money in your pocket. Once at work, do you use your own car to get around? You can claim the mileage as a tax deduction. You cannot claim the miles to and from home or to lunch unless it is a business lunch. Classic deductions are union dues, uniforms, professional licenses and dues, continuing education, reference and text books, job search. Do you work at home? Are you on call? You may be able to claim part of your cell phone and internet bill.

If your business is out of your home, such as a room is used as your business office, art studio or where you give massages or acupuncture then part of your rent or mortgage could be tax deductible.

Resume and Job Interview Tips

I have had the opportunity a couple of times to select new hires. I have had to sift through a hundred résumé's to pick five applicants to interview for a single opening. It was enlightening. Some of the things we are all told to worry about when applying for a job aren't necessarily correct.

What was I looking for? My focus was to hire somebody who could do the job with the shortest learning curve. I wanted somebody who would be happy doing the job. I didn't want to waste my time on an applicant that really wanted to do something else and would quit as soon as a better position came along.

Like everybody else in the room, interviewing job applicants was just another task on our overflowing plate. I just didn't have a lot of time to spend on it. I needed to get through the resume selection process quickly and fairly. This is how I determined the select few to interview.

Information that must be easy to find.

The resume needed to be typed. I didn't care what the layout was as long as it was organized. I wanted to know five things.

Your name. Surprisingly, this is not always easy to find! I didn't care about gender or ethnic group. I just needed to know what to call the applicant.

What degrees do you have, not what working towards. If you are still in school, when will you graduate? If you graduate before I need you to start, it's as good as having the degree. But failing to graduate on time would become a problem.

Who were your last employers and when? If there is a big gap in your employment, expect to be asked why, should you get an interview. There are a lot of acceptable reasons.

What types of work have you done in the past and for how long? Keywords are important. I have a job opening that needs certain skills. Those who have at least some experience needed would catch my attention. Those with the greatest number of hits on my wish list of skills became my favorite. If you do office work, what software packages do you know? Give me a list. If you are a software developer, what technologies have you used? The longer the list the better.

What kind of job do you want to do? If it is different than what you have been doing, state it. Do you want to be a project lead, program manager or a circuit designer? If you have been doing technical writing in your last job and don't state a desire, I will assume you want to do more of this.

What will hurt you?

Being vague or too wordy. It was frustrating trying to guess if an applicant had graduated or not and what their experience was. The resumes I had to read over and over all ended up in the reject stack. I just didn't have time to guess the answers to my five questions.

Some things don't matter.

Unless you are applying for a consulting firm that markets themselves as only having Harvard Grads, what college you graduated from only matters with your first job. After that, your work experience will define your career. If you get retrained for a new career, that's fine.

For entry level positions, I didn't expect the applicants to have experience. I was interested in what they'd studied in school. I wasn't after a class list but a skill list. Since I was hiring engineers and computer scientists, I wanted to know what languages and technologies they'd used. How many programs had they had written? What did each do? I wanted this all as lists and bullets. I didn't have time to read a novel.

Most interviewers rarely care about the clubs you are a member of. Clubs and hobbies that directly relate to the job being sought can be a way to show needed skills and bridge an extended period of unemployment.

Overstating your job experience can burn you in the interview. If you get hired as the subject matter expert and are not, expect to be fired. It's like telling your blind date that you are six foot tall when you are really five foot two. She's going to notice. The crime is fostering unrealistic expectations.

I was fine with the resumes being on ordinary paper. Expensive paper made no difference in my selections.

What will help you?

If you graduated from a prestigious school, you may have a fast track to the interview pile. It depends on the interviewer. At the worst, it doesn't hurt.

A past job somewhere exciting will get you attention. Who would you pick in the below two contests?

An intern worked on Wall Street verses a part time job at H&R Block.

Summer job at NASA verses four years part time at Radio Shack.

Let's face it, unless the rest of the resume has a lot more job opening related keywords key words in it, the sexier job experience will win out. The unsexy applicant may actually have better experience but at this point, it's hard to tell. Not to mention, an interviewer might be so fascinated with the space program that they'll give an interview to the ex-NASA intern just to hear some stories. It doesn't guarantee to be hired. The interviewer will be interviewing multiple people or each opening.

Interview Tips

1. Don't be too chatty.

Everybody being interviewed is on the hire list. This is still about shrinking the list to match the number of open positions. The interviewer is looking for reasons not to hire you. Saying less means fewer opportunities to put your foot in your mouth.

When you show up for the interview, keep this in mind. The interviewer is in charge. They have questions they want to ask. Let them ask what they need to know and reply clearly and briefly. Save your questions and any stories you might want to share until the end.

If this is a sales position, you want to seduce the interviewer. But know when to stop talking. I had a friend once who was a great salesman. He was always talking me into things. Somehow he would miss it when he had me sold. He'd keep talking and after a while, I'd always lose interest. You don't have to stay the whole time. Your interviewer has to eat lunch also.

2. No trouble makers allowed.

If this is a team position, do you come off as somebody who gets along with others?

If this is a management position, you want to show confidence without signs of being a bully.

3. Now your hobbies matter. Will you be happy in the new job?

You look better if you do something at home that relates to the job opening. If you volunteer at a soup kitchen and I want you to design a skyscraper, your hobby doesn't matter.

If the job opening is financial, you want to be able to say something like you dabble in stocks and do tax prep on the side. It doesn't have to be big money. If you have a passion for the subject field, you sound more likely to be able to learn the job quickly.

If you are applying to be a chef, do you like to cook at home? The answer had better be yes. Perhaps you e-published a cookbook? You don't have to have sold any. The mere act of have it for sale on Amazon.com will look very good.

On the flip side, if you are applying for a software development job but don't own a computer, you come off poorly.

Do you prefer working as part of a team or all alone? There are both kinds of jobs out there.

4. Above all be honest.

Never lie in an interview. If they don't ask, you don't have to tell.

14 Ways to become a favorite Employee

Getting your job done is often not always enough. Here are several tips how to help improve your standing at work and better position yourself for a promotion.

Get along. It doesn't matter how good you are at your job, if you are always fighting with somebody, management will get tired of having you around. The moment they realize they don't need you anymore, expect to get ejected.

Dress to fit in. Be part of the team. Hide the tattoos. Remove the face piercings. Work is the wrong place to make political statement. Dress like your boss. You can dress anyway you want outside of work.

What do you do that is annoying? Stop it. You don't have to look any further than the Dilbert comic strip to get a list of annoying stereotypes.

Don't talk too much. People are busy. When they ask you what time it is, don't first tell them the history of the clock. For some reason this usually becomes a problem with older people. I admit that I have been making this mistake too much as of late.

Be punctual.

Don't be invisible. You need to do a little bit of socializing or you'll become the forgotten employee. Doing a great job won't matter if the office is downsized. They'll have no emotional attachment to you. It'll be that much easier to put you on the layoff list. It'll also make it easy to forget you when promotions are being handed out.

Be polite and positive. Eating together is a powerful bonding technique. Look for an opportunity to bring donuts or a cake into work. There is always a birthday or holiday just around the corner.

Become the go-to guy. Whenever I start work in a new office, I learn the necessary little things that make the office work. For example, where do you get paper and ink when the photocopier runs out? I write up and hand out little cheat sheets on the common business processes everybody forgets. What form is used to request time off? How do you use the LaserJet printer as a scanner? Who do you call when the light bulb in the ceiling needs to be replaced? "I have the answer. Let me copy and paste it into an email for you."

Say, "Yes" to your boss instead of, "no". We've all seen it. There is always somebody at work that argues every time he is told to do something. The boss never appreciates a wrestling match. Simply saying, "Yes" to your boss can make you stick out as the easy one to work with.

When you tell the boss about a problem, always include a possible solution.

Volunteer for tasks you know you can succeed at.

Don't intentionally break any rules. It doesn't matter if you don't agree with the rules. They're handing you the paycheck. They get to make the rules. If something bugs you too much, you can always quit.

Be aware of politics enough to avoid it. Don't take sides. Don't allow yourself to become the fall guy. If your management is too out of control, quitting is best. They'll burn you sooner or later no matter what you do.

Take responsibility when you screw up. You may get punished but you'll get respect.

Turn your Home into Income

Your home is a classic example of something you own that can generate a lot of money. In general, you are selling your privacy. The effort you have to put into it can be small, with the extra income per month ranging from hundreds to thousands of dollars. There are several angles you can take advantage of. Hold onto your hat as we run through them.

My personal opinion is that if you are renting out a room, tenants that only plan to stay a year or two are best. Military, college students and recent graduates are examples. It gives you the easy option to eventually get your privacy back without having to evict.

When renting an entire home, tenants that may want to stay forever are the best. An example of this is a family with the bread earners in the same job for many years. Having an entire house vacant for months while you are hunting for new renters can be a big disruption. Besides the decrease in cash flow, you have a second house and yard to maintain.

I've combined several rental leases into one that satisfies my needs. If you don't have one, LegalZoom.com is a good source for contract. Their Real Estate Lease package has set of documents you may find useful.

I highly recommend going to your local library and reading the laws that govern rentals in your states. It won't be a long read. Expect about ten pages. There will be useful details in there that could save you grief later on. For example, you are not supposed to spend the security deposit. In many States when you return it to the departing tenant at the end of the lease you are supposed to include interest. I suggest you put the security deposit into a dedicated interest bearing account. Don't let it get mixed up with your savings.

When reading the laws, note what could cause you to lose your right to keep the security deposit. In Maryland, failure to do a walkthrough when the tenant moves in is just such an example.

Most of the time, even a renter can have a renter.

If you are a renter, you can may be able to make an extra buck if you are the sole occupant with an extra bedroom. Yes, take in a roommate. You'll need to vacate half the refrigerator, freezer and shelves in the kitchen. In exchange, expect the new roommate to pay half of the rent, gas and electric, cable, internet and phone bills. Since bedrooms are usually different sizes, whoever gets the master bedroom should pay a greater percentage of the rent.

You need to ask the landlord's permission in advance. They might get upset if they are surprised by a second tenant. Whether the roommate sublets from you (the renter) or they are added to the rental agreement is up to you and the landlord.

If they are added to the rental agreement, the landlord should state that you don't get evicted if the new person fails to pay the rent. This is the easiest option for you. You don't have to worry about handling security deposits and collecting the monthly rent. The down side is that the landlord will likely increase the rent because of the multiple occupancy. You'll see a savings but less than 50%. It might be a lot less. If you don't get along with the roommate, you won't be able to kick them out.

Landlords often prefer that you sublet. They restrict you to how many people are allowed. You are responsible for paying the rent and keeping the place in order. Collecting, holding and returning the security deposit is your responsibility. The advantage is you can kick the roommate out if there is trouble, and you'll maximize your savings.

Renting a room in your home as the owner.

If you are the owner of a condo, townhouse, or single family house you are the landlord. You can take in as many roommates as you like as long as you don't break any county occupancy laws or HOA (Home Owner Association) policies. In general you can have one adult per bedroom plus one. The best thing is that strangers are paying off part of you mortgage! If you are single, you are crazy not to do this for at least a couple of years.

The best homes to take in a roommate or two are the ones where there is a physical separation. For example, you have your bedroom and full bathroom on one floor. The roommate(s) have their bedroom(s) and full bathroom(s) on a separate floor. The common areas are minimally the kitchen and living room. The private spaces are the bedrooms and perhaps the individual bathrooms. Sharing the garage or not is up to you. Adults that have to share bathrooms are unhappy adults. Each roommate needs their own bedroom, bathroom and equal share of the kitchen and the laundry. How many cars are we talking about? There needs to be parking space for all of the cars plus a visitor or two!

Being the landlord you get to split up the house anyway you see fit. When I did this years ago, the living room was common space. Whoever got to the TV and sofa first got the room. I had to have a TV in my bedroom, my private space.

It was a split foyer. My daughter and my bedrooms were on the upper floor. The renter's bedroom and bath room was on the lower floor. The family room had a fireplace. I decreed the family room to be a common space so I could use it when I wanted. The renter could decorate it themselves including using their living room furniture, giving them the illusion that they had their own living room.

I was careful to stipulate that they had to keep the common areas tidy at all times. Their bedroom could be a mess but their bedroom door had to be kept closed. Long term messes make me crazy.

Do you allow pets, smoking and overnight guests? It's up to you. Increase the security deposit if there will be pets. Denying and adult to have an overnight guest is an iffy thing to do. You don't want an unpaid extra roommate. But you also don't want to become your roommate's mother. It is difficult to determine what is and what is not acceptable. Minimally, it is very reasonable to not allow your renter to have people in the house when neither of you are not at home.

Rent a room part-time.

The next option is to rent out a room part time! This is straight forward if you live in a tourist area. You can rent it out by the night, week or month. The room needs to be tastefully furnished with none of your personal possessions in it. It is in effect a hotel room. If your city has a major annual event or convention, there may be annual high demand for a room to rent. In Annapolis Maryland the hotels sell in out in May for the graduation ceremonies at the Naval Academy. The whole summer is the hot season if you live near the ocean, close to a major beach.

The upside is that you can have your privacy most anytime you want to. The down side is that you will frequently have a new person in the house. Be sure your home owner's insurance cover's the home and all of your possessions. You may want the deductible to be low in case the house is damaged or you get robbed.

An electronic lock on the front door is a great idea. They cost about $100. Some models allow a guest's combo. You can change the security code at a moment's notice and can provide the code over the phone or by email.

If you don't want an electronic lock, you'll minimally want a door with a key lock and a deadbolt. Don't give the deadbolt key to the renter. The deadbolt is used if you suddenly have a situation and need to keep the current or ex-renter out. The front door lock should be replaced between each renter. It isn't a hard job. But constantly replacing the lock is not very feasible. A compromise is to have a few different door locks that you cycle through.

Your short term renter may be new to the area. A nice touch would be to have a collection of tourist brochures in the room, waiting for them when they arrive. You can get that at your local State visitor center. A list of directions to the closest restaurant, grocery store, post office and shopping mall would be appreciated.

If your renter is only going to stay a few days, look to hotels for ideas how to kick it up a notch. Go to Target, Walmart or Kmart and stock up on sample sized shampoo, hair conditioner, toothpaste and tooth brushes can be very appreciated by your weekend guest. Providing a home cooked breakfast is always welcome.

If you advertise through your friend network, life is simple. With the internet, you can find the renters, sign the rental papers and get a deposit from a distance. But a public exposure could bring unwanted and unexpected attention. What are your local ordinances? Some cities won't allow you to rent out a room by the day or the week without being designated a Bed and Breakfast. If so, you'll need licenses and inspections. You will need a sprinkler system and possibly stickers on the bedroom doors stating the fire exits, etc… Cooking for your renter may require an extra level of licenses and inspections.

The fines can be significant. On National Public Radio, 13 Feb 2013 there was a story of a man in New York that listed his spare bedroom on the website AirBnB.com. He rented it to a traveler for a weekend and made $300. He later was hit with a bill for $30,000 for running an illegal bed and breakfast. The lesson to be learned is that if you are renting for short periods and have a public exposure, you need to take the local laws very seriously. Happily, most people who advertise through Air B and B haven't had this terrible experience.

Finding renters.

Your friend network is a good way to find somebody responsible. Most of the time you'll have to advertise. One way is to hire a real estate agent. The fee is typically the first month's rent.

There are a lot of websites where you can advertise for free your room or house to rent. The most famous is CraigsList.org. When using one of these sites, keep your eyes pealed for scammers. They have been very active the past several years. Don't post the house address or your last name. Make the prospective tenant call you to get the address.

When we advertised one of our houses, our ad was cloned. The overseas scammers, duplicated our ad and posted it on the same websites. They reused our photos. The only thing they changed was to drop the price in half and the contact info to themselves.

Their game is to get prospective tenants to respond to their ad then pretend that they are you, the landlord. They tell the victim, "Don't worry about a credit check! I trust you. I am on vacation in Europe at the moment. Just give me your credit card to pay the security deposit and the first month's rent. Show up at the house and somebody will be there with the key to the front door."

Of course, they take the money and run. The clueless victim shows up at your front door, angry and demanding their money back. If this happens to you, report it to the police. They likely won't be able to catch the crooks but the police report will provide a serious defense should a victim try to sue you for the lost money.

How to spot the scammers yourself? Check the popular websites on a daily basis and notify the system administrators immediately if you see your ad cloned. If you get a suspicious phone call or your ad gets cloned, you can put on your detective hat. You can look up the area code on the internet to determine where the phone may be calling from. Another is a reverse phone number look up.

Reverse number lookup at WhitePages.com
Area code lookup at WhitePages.com

Sites to advertise on:

ApartmentGuide.com
CraigsList.org
EasyRoommate.com
ForRent.com
Rent.com
RoommateLocator.com
Vrbo.com
Zillow.com

Background checks.

The easiest way to run a credit check is an online credit service to check the credit of prospective renters. TenantBackgroundSearch.com, landlordStation.com and tentantVerification.com are just a few. These charge about $25 per credit check. Have the applicant pay for it.

You have the choice whether to accept the unlikely but potentially edited copy or insist on a new report. Wisconsin is one of the States that requires that you accept the copy if it is less than 30 days old. Since the renter may need to apply to several places before being accepted, it is cost effective for them to pay this credit report fee once and print out copies to hand out. By law, all of us are allowed to get a free credit report on ourselves once a year. The three credit bureaus are Experian, TransUnion and Equifax. Using one at a time, waiting several months between, you can have a fresh report three times a year!

The credit report will tell you if they pay their bills on time, have been evicted, or have filed for bankruptcy. In some States would tell you if they had been convicted of a crime.

The FICO score is the person's over all grade. It is between 300 and 850. 650 is a medium risk.

Each State has their court cases online. You can search for be displayed the court records of the prospective tenant. It will tell if they have been convicted of crime or changed their name. The categories are typically Civil, Criminal, Traffic, Civil Citation or all. States like Maryland and Florida are free. Colorado charges a small fee per search while Florida's fee is more significant.

To find this website for your State, Google the search term, "Judiciary Case Search" including the State of interest. There are plenty of middleman websites such as instantCheckmate.com. However, I have found that they miss a lot. You are better going straight to the State websites. If the person has a common name, it will be a challenge determining which one in the long list is your applicant.

Each State has their sex offender registry on-line. Google the key words "sex offender registry" adding the State of interest. If there is a hit on your applicant's name, it'll include a photo.

Is your house or property next to a stadium?

If your home is next to a busy venue with limited parking like an opera house or stadium, you may be able to rent out your driveway or yard as event parking. Growing up, I used to see this in my home town. There wasn't enough parking at the stadium for all of the spectators. The owners at some of the houses would stand outside on Sundays before the football games with signs stating how much it would cost to park in their front yard and driveways. For some, it was an easy hundred dollars a week.

In another city, I know about a popular bar that didn't have enough parking. There was no parking on the busy road in front of it, limiting the number of customers. Just a couple of buildings away was a house with a double lot. If I had been the home owner, I would have considered trying to swing a deal with the bar owner. For a fee from the bar, part of my large property could be used as overflow parking.

Do you have extra storage space?

Do you have a floored attic, large shed or large parcel of land? Opportunities often present themselves unexpectedly. You could rent out any of these for long term storage. I once had a friend who was going to move half of her things into a storage bin for a couple of years. I let her store it at my place for half the price. But if you do this, be prepared to allow them easy access to their stuff.

Home Owner Associations rarely allow boats to be parked at the owner's homes. In some cases, there just is no parking to be had. If you have an easily accessible parcel of land, you could be the answer to their prayers. Marinas can be expensive. Charging half the going rate to park a boat on a trailer will find you easy money during the winter months.

Do you have something special like a pier?

A pier is easy to rent out. Slips are expensive. You could make a thousand a year without breaking a sweat. The key thing you also have to have is extra parking. During the summer, expect to have one or two cars parked at your house every nice weekend. Also expect your renter to want to use the garden hose to wash the boat and the bathroom once in a while. If you can provide an outdoor power outlet and water faucet at the pier, you can charge a higher rate. Want to kick it up? How about a picnic table next to the pier and a small shed they can use.

Build a Real Estate Empire!

This option is about renting out an entire house. If you rent out your first house, you need a second one to live in. If you don't have a second house this is a way to get one quickly. First, fill the extra bedrooms of your home with roommates. With the extra income, buy a second house. When you move into it, rent out the bedroom you left behind. If you are ambitious, get roommates for your new house. When you are comfortable, buy a third house and rent out the bedroom you left behind in the second house.

Since you are always buying your primary residence, you will always get the best interest rate from the banks and have to put down the minimum deposit. Over the course of several years you will be in command of a lot of real estate. Best yet, other people are paying your mortgages!

If you want to buy a second home but not move into it, the key detail is for it to be a "vacation home". If you call it an "investment property" the bank will charge you a higher interest rate and require a larger down payment. Be wary about renting out the vacation house all year around, at least in the first couple or few years. The banks will get upset if they catch you.

Mid sized houses are the best to collect. The neighborhoods are more likely to be appealing than the bottom end houses. The capital gains on high end Mc-Mansions can grow the fastest but can be very hard to sell if you suddenly need to. Also, charging rent that is triple that of a two bedroom apartment filters out most of the renting population. Most people that have this kind of money to spend want to buy a house, not rent.

An exception to this rule would be if your goal is to quickly resell the house for a profit. Flip it. Builders sometimes use this strategy. They build a house with the intention of moving in. The house goes on the market as soon as it is convent. They both work their way up to a more luxurious home for their family and have lower loan cost from the bank.

When house hunting keep a few things in mind. Houses need maintenance. If you don't know how to make repairs you'll have to pay somebody to do it. Seek out a good handyman for the jobs you can't or don't want to do yourself. Check with your local power company. It has become popular for them to provide maintenance plans. For a little as $40 a month, you can cover the air conditioning, furnace, stove, oven and refrigerator, washer and dryer. If anything breaks, the tenant can call the power company who will send out a repair man to fix it at no cost.

You don't want your growing collection of houses in the same neighborhood. If the neighborhood goes bad, your entire real estate portfolio will suffer. Nor do you want them scattered all around the country. It will become unmanageable. You need to be able to get to most of your homes in a reasonable amount of time. I prefer an hour drive or less. There have been several occasions where I have had to drive to one after work, several days in a row to do repairs and inspections.

When you buy a house remember, location, location, location. Who are the major employers in your area? The house needs to be a reasonable distance from where your likely renters will go to work or school. You want to be no more than twenty minutes from the local military base, government offices, colleges, or factories. The schools need to be good. The Crime needs to be low. You don't want to be on a busy street. It needs to be a quiet neighborhood so don't buy homes that are next to airport runway or on a busy street.

How old is the roof, furnace, water heater and air conditioning? They are expensive to replace. Furnaces and central air conditioning units last about 20 years. Heat pumps lat about eleven years. They cost about $5,000 to replace. A water heater will last about 18 years. A roof will last about 20 years. A good idea is to use a permanent marker and write on the side of the water heater and furnace the date installed and the expected replacement date. This is especially important with water heaters. They rust out from the inside. Replace it before it goes otherwise one day you'll have a flooded house.

Next you want the house to have at least one thing special and nothing wrong with it. Look for a wow factor! Something special can be a simple as being within walking distance to shopping or happening hangouts. Does the back yard have privacy or a nice view? Is there plenty of parking? A pool can be either a wow or a problem. Pools need maintenance. An above ground pool or hot tub can be thrown away. An in-ground pool is expensive if not kept up. A neighborhood with amenities such as a pool, or a park, located close to a shopping mall are all selling features. Beyond the obvious, you will sell the house someday. A good house will sell even in a bad market.

You want one thing special and nothing wrong

My first house was a baggy. It was poor of quality and small. In short, it was very inexpensive. When it was time to sell, I didn't have a problem. Buyers would try to get me into price wars with the neighbors. There were about fifty identical duplexes in the neighborhood. At any time there were ten for sale. Why should I get top dollar for mine? Mine was special. I had the largest yard. It was fenced, great for buyers with big dogs and little children. I had extended the driveway so one could have two cars off the road. I had added a doorbell though the glass top stove was the real eye catcher for the couple that bought the house.

Redfin.com - To find what houses are for sale in the area you are interested in.

Zillow.com - How much is the house and its neighbors are worth. You also get the historical curve. If the house has an addition, or major upgrade, Zillow might not know about it.

AreaVibes.com - Provides stats about the neighborhood, the local population's local income, nearby amenities, and rates the local schools. The crime stats can give you an inaccurate feeling an area is worse than really is. Recommend you enter your current address first to get a sense of what the stats really mean.

CrimeReports.com - This site shows you a map with icons representing where crimes of various times have occurred. It also shows where the sex offenders live along with a picture of their face. This site's data is comprehensive for some cities and lacking in others.

You can rent a vacation house part-time.

A vacation house is for you to vacation in. If the bank gets wind of you renting it out full time, you could get in trouble. However, by definition, you are only vacationing part of the year. You can rent it out the rest of the year. And a vacation house is expected to be located in a vacation area.

As with turning your home into a bed and breakfast, check the local ordinances. The fines can be significant. You may need sprinkler systems, stickers on the bedroom doors stating the fire exits, etc...

Since the vacation home is likely too far for you to drive there every week to clean between renters, mow the lawn, hand out the house key and in general keep an eye on the place, you'll need a manager. This can be a local friend or family member. If you don't have one, you can hire a property manager through the local real estate office. Some may even advertise for you, keeping the furnished house rented during the months you don't plan on being on vacation. Shop around for a manager to get the best deal.

Loaning money and renting a house to relatives is always a risky business. But sometimes it works out. Our boys grew up move across the country and just starting their adult lives out, they combined their pay checks and rented apartment together. Their rent was $1000 a month. Around the same time, my wife and I bought a vacation home in the same area. It was a "short sale" so we got a great deal on the four bedroom single family house. The mortgage was about $1000 a month. After a year the boy's apartment increased to $1200 a month. The vacation house was costing less than their apartment! And the house was an investment unlike the apartment.

To cut costs, the boys ultimately moved into the home. After a time, they brought in two roommates whose combined rent covered the mortgage. The boys ended up having both a much nicer place to live by moving into the house and by taking in room mates were rent free! With the freed up income, in time they will start collecting houses of their own.

What to do with an empty lot.

Several buildings down from the popular bar I previously mentioned was another empty lot. When major road work was needed, it was leased out as a temporary parking and staging area for the earth movers and storage for the construction material.

Common enough, you see such lots used to sell Christmas trees in December. How to find somebody to rent the lot from you? You can advertise on a website like <u>Craigslist.com</u> or you can talk to the merchants selling trees at Christmas. Ask them how much they pay. Perhaps you can entice them to move to your lot for a lower lease.

Keep and eye out for squatters. People selling plants and Christmas trees on vacant lots next to major roads don't always have permission to be there.

What to do with empty land.

If you have a large acreage of land, opportunities open up depending on the size and location. In the 1960's my father bought 130 acres of farmland on the Maryland Eastern shore. He had hopes that the second Bay Bridge was going to be built across the Chesapeake Bay to Taylor Island. If so, the land would be worth a fortune.

He held on to it for decades. The old farm returned to forest. Alas, the second Bay Bridge ended up being built next to the first one up at Annapolis. Instead of letting the land sit, he rented it out to deer hunters. It more than paid the annual property tax. In the 2000's he finally sold it for much more than he had originally paid for it and used the money to build a house out West.

In the 1990's, I had wanted to up his income. One idea was to log the center. A lumber company would come in and clear what I desired, paying Dad for the trees. Lush grass would grow, feeding the deer. More deer would then make the land better hunting.

With the center 80 acres cleared, we could them lease the land to dirt bikers and ATV's outside of the hunting months. You can see how one idea can build on another.

- Billboards if next to a highway
- Cell tower
- Hunting & fishing
- Logging

Energy companies are hunting for natural gas. They send a pipe underground into the shale deposited and break them up, release and collecting the gas. This pays the land own very well. The risk is of possible ground water contamination. This can damage the environment and make the property worthless.

If the land is next to a farm, you could lease it to the farmer for growing crops.

There was a farm in the Midwest that I used to visit when I was in college. Dump trucks from nearby construction areas would haul in dirt and dump it on the property. The Farmer got paid per truck load. This had obviously been going on for several years as the dirt was piled up into a fairly tall and long hill. It may have been fifty feet tall and a hundred feet long with a graceful but steep slope. Being in a part of the country devoid of mountains, it was a popular hill for people to learn how to fly hang gliders.

Income Taxes

Splitting the rent with a roomy has no tax implications. Renting out a room in your house is taxable. But renting out an entire house can easily be

$20,000 or more a year of income. If you don't claim it on your taxes and the IRS finds out, you can end up in prison. At the least you'll be looking at a very expensive fine. If you do claim it, depending on your tax bracket you may be paying as much as a third of this in taxes at the end of the year.

But wait! This is a business model. You are doing this to make a profit. Thus you can deduct business expenses on your taxes. What can you deduct? Keep the receipts for all repairs. You can't count the labor hours unless somebody else did the job and billed you for it.

What else can you deduct? You can deduct the Home Owner's insurance, Home Owner's Association dues, Maintenance policies, sewer assessment fee, front footage fee and mileage to travel to check up on the house. These are all business expenses. If there is a pool or an in-ground sprinkler system in the yard? You can deduct the cost to open the pool in the Spring and to winterize them both in the Fall.

Do you need a license to rent a house?

If you are a property manager, the answer is almost universally yes. You need either a real estate broker or manager license.

If you are the home owner then it depends on the county and city. Usually the owner doesn't need a license, permit or "Rental Housing Certificate" if less than three homes are being rented. If the house is in a neighborhood with an HOA (Home Owner's Association) there may be a clause banning renting out the home. In some communities in Minnesota, there is a limit to the total number of houses that can be for rent at the same time.

Here is a summary of most of United States. It is not 100% complete and this information is subject to change over time. A good alternative summary is AllPropertyManagement.com/propertylaw/. Use either of these lists as a quick reference but not a substitute for contacting your local city hall.

If you are the owner, you do not need a license if the house your are renting is in Arizona, California, Florida, Georgia, Michigan, Mississippi, Montana, Nevada, New Hampshire, New Jersey, New Mexico, North Dakota, Ohio, Oregon, Rhode Island South Carolina, South Dakota, Utah or Wyoming. In California you don't need a license but you may need a inspection to certify that the house is habitable.

In Florida, the theme is no license needed as long as the rental is longer than 30 days. It also applies to a single room. Renting by the day or week in most States is part of the definition of Bed and Breakfast.

In Minnesota, the answer is most often yes, you need a "Rental Housing Certificate.

Washington State it depends on the city and county. Likewise in Virginia, Aurora Illinois, and Boulder Colorado expect to need a Housing Rental License.

A quick look at Pennsylvania and the answer is that part of the State does, and part doesn't. Philadelphia and Lebanon require the rental units be

registered and inspected. Pittsburg requires both a
Certificate of Occupancy and a housing rental permit.

In Maryland you don't have to for much of the
State. The ones that you need a license are: The city
of Cumberland, City of Annapolis, Baltimore City,
Baltimore County, Howard County, Montgomery
County, Prince Georges County, the city of Salisbury.
Ocean City requires a business license. Dorchester
County does not require a license but rental units
must be registered.

Getting started buying stocks

Are you wanting to buy stocks but not sure how to get started? This series of articles is to give the sort of 101 lecture about the stock market that my father never gave to me.

Once you were paying your bills and have some extra money to save for a rainy day where you put it is the big question. You start with the safest place you can find. This is a savings account. Savings and loans pay a higher interest rate than a bank. Unless inflation is high, both pay almost nothing. But you are guaranteed that it won't shrink. Where this can go wrong is if you are charged fees for the account to exist. Demanding a minimal balance exists, avoid institutions that charge you fees for a savings account merely to exist.

You should have a few a few thousand dollars in a savings account. My rule of thumb is enough to cover three emergencies. How much money it takes to cover a financial emergency depends on your financial life. An emergency could be a car repair, a month's rent or a new water heater.

The next step is to put some money away that has a higher rate of return and almost a safe. A CD is a common choice. Like a savings account, you put money away in a CD with no risk of that shrinking. The problem is that you are locking it away for some period of time. If you pull it out early, you forfeit the interest gained in that period of time. The next step is to either buy real estate, typically a house or Stocks. Each has its own set of advantages and hassles. Over time, you want both to whatever degree makes you happy.

There are many ways to play stock market. They range from simple, safe and cautious too fast and very high-risk. The latter is a akin gambling and should never be attempted by a novice. This is where people gaining more often lose fortunes overnight.

How much money do you need to buy stock?

If using a stockbroker you need at least $2000 a buy. This is because the fees are relatively high. You pay a fee when you buy and again when you sell. You need to buy a larger amount of stock a time for your profits to cover fees. E*TRADE or Ameritrade are effectively the same as a stock broker without the personal attention thus half or less of the fees. After the crash of 2000 they started charging fees if you didn't buy and sell often enough. That's when I stopped dealing with them.

Mutual funds require $1000 or $50 a month until you reach the minimum balance. This amount varies depending on the fun. It looks and feels like a savings account. Your money is combined with thousands of other people. Without talking to you, Stockbrokers (fund managers) buy and sell stock across one or more industries rather than a single stock. The fees vary drastically from fund to fund. Morningstar reports are one page long with everything you want to know and long with how each is rated. You can get up to date reports for free at the public library reserve desk.

DRIPS require $250 or $50 a month until you reach the minimum balance. It looks and feels like a savings account. This amount varies depending on the fund. Like using a stockbroker, E*TRADE or Ameritrade you buy one stock at a time. The fees are much lower because you bypass the stockbroker and buy directly from the company that issued the stock. Large companies are the only ones that offered DR IP accounts.

How do you make a profit?

The simple answer is dividends and capital gains. If the company makes a profit, they usually give some of it to the stockholders as dividend payments. You get a check in the mail one to four times a year. With DRIPS and mutual funds, this can be auto-reinvested to buy more of the same stock.

Capital gains is the stock price increasing value after you bought it. You intend to buy low and someday sell for a high price. You turn a "potential" profit into a "real" profit when you sell the stock. Companies that pay high and regular dividends are rarely ones that change in value very fast.

What is Risk?

Risk is a measure of volatility in an the aspect of the stock. Typically this typically referring to the share price. A low risk stock would have a stable stock price or always pays dividends.

What is a stock split?

A stock split it like making change for a dollar. You're one share of stock that is worth $100 is replaced with two shared each worth $50. So why do people get excited about a split? The pattern is that most stock that splits returns to it's previous value in about two years. In other words, there is a reasonable chance you will double your money in two years.

Strategies

There are countless strategies for selecting what stock to buy and when to buy it. One buying strategy based on only buying stocks that announced a split. Google "stock splits" and the current year. The expectation is that you'll double your money in two years. Exxon is one of my long time favorites. Exxon split a few times since I have owned it. The share price would reach $100 then it would spilt into two $50 shares (2:1 split). They would increase to $100 then split again and again.

The safest strategy is called dollar-cost average. Once you select the stock, buy a fixed amount on the schedule. For example, buy $100 worth on the first of every month. Some months you pay too much. Other months you'll get a great deal. On average, you'll be paying a reasonable price. Coupled wit h this, is the goal to buy and hold the stock for at least five years. However, if the stock is found to under perform for a year or two compared to the market, it is okay to sell it and move your money to a better performing stock.

One interesting strategy is to follow specific CEO's careers. Occasionally there is a Chief Executive Officer whose every touch turns to gold. Buy the companies they get hired by and sell quickly if the leave. Google "Best CEOs'".

Following trends in the market by following individual stock prices, the DOW and S&P 500, whether fast or slow is the most common theme. Is the stock value rising consistently over time? Is the dividend paid out every quarter for the past few years? Are there any countries melting down financially, potentially causing others to become shaky?

What is the DOW?

The DOW (DOW Jones Industrial Average) is a list of 30 stocks first created by Charles DOW in 1896. The theory was that by tracking the performance of the top companies, the health and trends of the whole stock market could be seen. Today, what companies that are on the list is determined by S&P Dow Jones Indices owned by McGraw-Hill Financial.

Since being on the list means by many measures, the company is the best of the best, one stock picking strategy is to only buy DOW companies. Another is to only buy the DOW dogs. These are the ten DOW stocks that pay the most Dividends.

Other prominent indexes are the S&P 500, Wilshire 5000, Russell 2000. The NASDAQ Composite tracks 3000 companies.

Tracking multiple stocks

A stock can catch you eye in many ways from heavy research of many companies across and industry to over hearing a stock tip in the hallway. But once a company has caught your attention you want to know the basics. Many web pages will give you stock quotes. E*trade, Ameritrade and Scott trade will give you stock quite without first opening an account.

One of the things to look at is the stock value trend. The default is usually one day. Take a look at all of settings. The 1 day setting is only good for day trading. To see the larger trends the one year average may be of more use. These slower cycles are easier for a the beginner to spot and take advantage of.

Another major detail to look at is the average dividend yield. If you want the lottery or inherited a lot of money, you may want to buy large quantities of stock and live off the quarterly dividends. This way the initial investment is never touched except maybe during a recession, when dividends may shrink for a year or two.

Of the list of stocks that have caught your eye, you need an easy way to track and compare their progress. only some of the stock quote web pages will do this. Try entering in the list of stock ticker names separated by a comma. Two web pages that do are Flash Quotes and Scott Trade.

Different kinds of trends

Getting a stock quote an looking at the historical trend may show a repeated oscillation of a stock. It might be seasonally. An propane company may make most of it's profit in the winter so it would deep in value in the summer. In this case, summer is when you'd want to buy. If a harsh winter is predicted, you might want to buy a greater amount of stock. If a hurricane damages refineries in Texas, the stock price may rise fast and early because of a predicted gas shortage.

Fear and anxiety drive the market

If something occurs to cause a stock price to plummet but doesn't endanger the future of the company, you have an unexpected opportunity to make a quick profit. When Steve Jobs went public that his cancer was back, Apple share price dropped to half. But once the market realized that even if he died on et spot, the company was healthy and had enough products in the works to keep it a major innovator for at least a couple more years. The stock price recovered a couple of days later.

A recession is when
your neighbor is out of work

Recessions are a great opportunity to make a profit assuming you have cash on hand. It is a good strategy to have a war chest on the side for such an event. There is no universally accepted definition so this is as good as any. A recession is a twenty percent- kicked off by a major event such as the 1997 Asian financial crisis triggered an economic recession.

The 2000 recession (Y2K) occurred because of the fear of the Y2K bug. About 1997, efforts to modernize commercial, military and banking software to fix the bug started in earnest. In many cases, new computers were bought. When January first, 2000 happened, much of the world's corporations had modernized their computer system. They stopped spending. The armies of computer scientists and administrators had finished their Y2K task, and suddenly unemployed. By 2002, industry's need to regularly replace and upgrade their computers and network infrastructure had returned to normal.

A depression is when you are out of work

A depression is a more extreme recession. It is a fifty percent decrease in the stock market and last for four to ten years. The collapse of the housing market in Sept 2008 hit bottom by summer of 2009. Since then the market started to recover. Many otherwise healthy stocks like Ford and Discover Card were also hot pretty hard. I made a guess when we were close to the bottom and bought Ford. It fell a little farther then rebounded. I held the stock a couple of months longer than I intended then sold, doubling my money. Six years after the crash, I still have my Discover Card. My potential profit as of last week was 628%. I think I'll hold the stock a little longer.

Whenever you decide to buy,
it is the wrong time

The intention is to buy low and sell high. But what often makes one want to buy a stock is because it has had a long upward run. Nothing can go up forever. Once you see the tend, it often is too late to catch the wave. The real skill is buying when a stock is on the way down but for temporary reasons. Blue light special in isle three!

The fees are always a key detail

In part one, I mention some of the ways to make money off the stock market. In part to, provide some strategies to pick stocks. In this one, I give advice how to minimize your fees, maximizing your profit or minimizing your losses.

Making money is like hunting.
The prey doesn't want to be caught.

When I first started buying stocks, I use the dollar-cost average method. I also looked for month long cyclical trends. When I had a little extra money, I would buy stock when there were easy to spot dips. In general, I held and rarely sold. It was like collecting baseball cards. Instead of spending any extra money that was burning a hole in my pocket on a whim gadget, I spend it on Whim stock. Once every year or two I'd compare the performance of each stock, selling the dogs, putting the money into my best performers, maybe adding a new stock to the list. Over four years, I had more money compiled than I had expected.

Before you buy your first stock, you need to determine the fee to buy, to sell and to hold the stock. If the fees are too high, you need to make that much more on a trade to turn a profit. Or, buy more shares of stock at a time. A stockbroker will charge you the most to buy and sell but shouldn't charge you an annual fee to hold the shares. The minimum amount to spend on a trade ends up being about $2000. In the depths of a recession after the market has fallen 20%, $1000 might work as a minimal purchase amount.

The most cost-effective mutual funds are called "no – load" funds. They typically charge nothing to buy, a small amount to sell and typically 1% annually to hold. If they grow 10% a year, the 1% fee isn't bad when compared to what you get these days for a CD or savings account. A mutual fund the charges above 1% is expensive. One advantage of a mutual fund is that dividends can be used to automatically buy of stock. You can even buy partial shares making every penny count. Although the minimum balance is typically to thousand $2500. If you make monthly purchases of as little is $50 you meet the minimum balance, you don't need the $2500 upfront.

There are at least 10,000 mutual funds. I used to go to the library and page through the reference copy of the Morning Star. I'd photocopy the page on each of the few best funds, go home and study the stats. Recommend going right to their list of the best performers. Off the fund reports, I'd get the 800 number to call and get it an application form. Now a days these forms can be downloaded from the Internet.

DRIPs, sometimes called "no-load" funds are the single stock equivalent of a mutual fund. This can be the least expensive way to Buy a stock. It is set up the same as a mutual fund but the minimum balance is typically $250. The minimum purchase is $50. Just like a mutual fund, as long as you make monthly purchases a $50 until you meet the minimum balance, you don't need the $250 up front.

The low fees make of this in my opinion a great low-cost way to get started with the stock market. It also is best to use a dollar-cost average strategy. Make a purchase using a fixed amount on a monthly basis perhaps as a payroll deduction. Over time they should have much more money then you would if it has sat in a savings account or CD.

A few stocks that can be bought as DRIPS are Exxon, Proctor and Gamble, Merck, Kellogg and Kraft. For an extensive list, google, DRIPs, dividend reinvestment plan, or no-load stocks. Some of the websites with free lists are www.dripcentral.com, www.noload.info and www-us.computershare.com. Some of there lists are old but much of the information should still be valid.

Make Money from your Hobby

Turning your hobby into a source of income can be an exciting adventure. You already spend as many hours doing it as you can manage. So, it is kosher to not use the minimal wage rule when figuring if the work is worthwhile. Any amount is good. The goal is to creep up over time, how much you make an hour.

The problem with collectables is that it can be hard to know what will be of value many years in the future when you are ready to sell. Collectables like comic books and baseball cards were all the rage for about twenty years. The bottom dropped out when the manufacturers flooded the market.

Why not collect gold, gems and money as a hobby?

If just starting out, why not collect the old fashioned way. I am talking about gold, silver and gems. You of course want to buy when the market is low. There was a relative low in 1985 then 2001. In 2011, gold prices were at a historical high ($1571 per troy ounce). If you wait, it will drop in price again.

Collecting money can be fun. U.S. dollar bills have a different look over the years. Ever see a 1920 twenty dollar bill? How about a two dollar bill? A gold certificate? A silver certificate? At coin shops you can get inexpensive books to hold pennies, nickels, dimes and quarters. Try to find one from each mint going back to before World War II. Many are still in circulation. Every State has its own quarter. These are fun to seek out. How about silver half dollars and dollar coins? Years later if you ever need it, you have a box of money to fall back on! My father threw pennies into a couple large containers for decades. One day he hauled them to the bank and used the money to buy a new outboard motor for his small boat.

This doesn't work very well with foreign money. Unlike the US, most countries re-issue their currency every so many years making the old money worthless. I found it out the hard way when I was overseas. For the first time, the US Treasury made a drastic change in the look of the twenty dollar bill. Not thinking, I had older twenties with me. I had a very hard time spending them. I was accused of trying to spend worthless money! Most didn't believe me that I wasn't trying to con them. Their reality didn't include being able to spend currency that was fifty years old.

Sell what you make

Starting a hobby just to make a profit is rarely cost effective. Recall my earlier story about the gentleman with the chickens in his backyard? But if you already have something going, it's worth a shot.

My father was a great backyard farmer. He had a couple fruit trees and was passionate about growing vegetables. For a couple of years when I was around five or six years old, I would fill my red wagon up with fifty or sixty apples from his trees and knock on the neighbor's doors and sell them. I'm work my way all the way around the block. My success was more than being a cute little kid. These were grocery store quality apples. But what is the adult equivalent?

Turning your back yard into a toy farm just to sell fruits and vegetables at a farmer's market would be more money and effort than is reasonable. But if you have already done this and have a large quantity of good quality fruits and vegetables, selling them at the occasional farmer's market could be a fun way to make some extra money.

The farmer's market will have a manager. Contact this person to find out the cost to set up a tent and table. They also can tell you if you need a license to sell raw fruits and vegetables. The answer will be different depending on the city, county and State. But if the produce is cooked in any way, you will definitely need a license, a food handling certificate and much more.

With organic foods all the rage, getting yourself certified would be a great selling point, and increase the amount you could charge. According to the EPA's website, "Organically grown" food is food grown and processed using no synthetic fertilizers or pesticides. Pesticides derived from natural sources (e.g., biological pesticides) may also be used in producing organically grown food."

"Beginning on October 21, 2002, producers and handlers must be certified by a USDA-accredited certifying agent to sell, label, or represent their products as "100 percent "organic," "organic," or "made with organic (specified ingredients or food group(s)." For more information, go to the USDA's National Organic Program webpage.

If you love to make arts and crafts, you can rent a table at an arts and craft show or a flea market. You could also teach how to make your favorite creations. You could make You Tube videos teaching how to make each craft and collect ad revenue.

Planes and boats.

Do you have a pilot license or are an avid sailor (sailboat)? Since you already have the knowledge and experience, you could teach a class. Many marinas offer sailing classes.

I knew a gentleman who became friends with a marina owner. The marina wanted to expand the services it provided. The boat owner offered guidance and assistance that evolved into being asked to teach a class once in a while. He enjoyed it. He ended up creating his own class materials, diagrams, cheat sheets and hand outs.

He told me how much he enjoyed it but it was a hassle going to the copy shop to print out copies of his booklets for his students. It was one task that he would procrastinate on. I told him that if I was in his shoes, I'd take all of the papers and publish them on a website that did Publish On Demand (POD). I prefer the website CreateSpace.com.

With POD, no copies exist until they are ordered. Then, just that number of books are professionally printed. Create Space charges nothing and takes a cut of the profit when copies are sold. With this set up, all he'd have to do it tell the students to buy a copy off of Amazon.com. Or if he preferred, he could go online and order a stack for each class and hand them out to the students on their first day.

Being the book is for sale on Amazon.com, strangers will see it and might buy the occasional copy.

Water sports

If you live on the water and have a jetski or sailboard, you could rent it out. You'd need little more than a sign on the road side and a credit card reader for your iPhone and an account. The "Square Credit Card Reader" is about $11.

MacMall Part number: 972087
Manufacturer Part number: R01A1W

Art and Photography

If you have experience editing videos and low on income, you can save money by making your wedding present a video of their special day. If done well, this could be used as advertising to film others for a fee.

Photography can go in a couple of directions. If your photos are artistic, you can make good quality prints of your favorite photographs. Put them in frames and enter them in local contests. Maybe you'll sell a few pieces.

When I was in my artist stage, I did charcoal drawings. I won people's choice in a contest and sold a couple pieces. At my height, a gallery on the

Eastern Shore carried several drawings. I learned inexpensive ways to make small quantities of prints. It was an adventurous couple of years. Ultimately, it ended because my hobby had become a chore. I found myself spending more time trying to sell than doing what I enjoyed, trying to capture beauty on paper. This is your biggest risk when trying to make money off your hobby.

You can sell your digital images on-line through sites like BigStockPhoto.com. You can make about $3 or more a sale. This website screens the submissions, filtering out the poorer ones. They look for images with strong technical quality. They already have plenty of flowers, cats, and mountains. They are searching images of professional quality with a general appeal. Most of the buyers are looking for conceptual images for use in ad campaigns, business presentations and book covers.

The images should be 300 DPI with "fine" compression. In general, the greater the mega pixel the better. From their website, the average photo dimension is 2400 pixels on the longest side. Image file sizes can be up to 25 MB. The larger images (4000 pixels wide and greater) sell for higher prices.

Dude we're getting the band back together!

Do you dream of being a stand up comedian? Are you in a band or solo, do you play most any kind of instrument or sing? More importantly, are you any good? Do strangers like the sound you make? If you are good and not making money from it, there are several options short of quitting your job and making a go at it full time.

How to determine if you are good enough? Film yourself and post it on You Tube. It's not hard as I will describe later on in this book. Don't stand in your messy bedroom and sing into the camera. Ham it up and have fun. Try to make your own music video. Later on, you may want to use it as part of your resume when you are trying to land paying gigs.

People on You Tube will be brutally honest. Sometimes too brutal. But if you get a lot of hits over the course of a couple months, you may have real potential. Just in case you get a million hits in a year, post an ad on it so you'll get paid.

The next step is to seek out open mic night. They are mainly at bars and lounges. This is not the same as karaoke. And you won't get paid but it will give you experience performing in front of an audience. Continue with this until you feel comfortable. The challenge may be to match the type of music you do with what the audience is expecting. If it is a Jazz bar, they won't like country western or opera.

The next step is to enter a talent contest. Try googling "Talent show" in your area. In Baltimore, one such contest is called "The Big Show." Talent shows and contests normally charge a fee to compete. Again you won't get paid but it will be additional exposure and practice entertaining an audience.

Be sure to film both your open mic night and talent show performances. Watch it over and over, looking for ways to improve. Do you work the audience or stand there like a house plant? Are you loud enough or do the instruments drown you out. If your performance is good enough, post them on You Tube. You may be on your way to becoming a local celebrity. And don't forget to put an ad on your videos.

At this point you'll know if it is time to try to get a paying job performing at a bar, restaurant or audience. Would you be appropriate for a wedding or graduation party? There are all kinds of bars, Country Western, Rock, and Jazz. If you love to play Polka music seek out German restaurants, especially during October Fest! If you are into whaling songs and sea shanties, you can hunt a gig at a seafood restaurant or marina. Does the local sailing crown have an annual Pirates weekend raft up? Renaissance festivals need performers.

The last idea is to put out an album. You need good recording equipment. If you can accomplish this, you can go through CreateSpace.com to publish your music or comedy act on CD or as an MP3 download. It'll be for sale on Amazon.com. Buy some copies to resell when you perform at that bar or restaurant!

Do you do something exotic?

How about acting? Ever wish you could land a part in a movie? You know, something for a few hours on a Tuesday night or the weekend? You don't have to live in Hollywood for New York to have a shot at being an extra. A lot more movies and TV shows are filmed in the Baltimore/Annapolis/DC triangle that you'd expect. Years ago I was part of the crowd in a couple of the stadium scenes in the movie

Major League II. It was a fun evening. I got to be in the freshly built Orioles stadium before it was open to the public for the first time. I had a experience and no I didn't get paid.

But some extras do get paid. One way to find out about these opportunities is calls for extras is online. Google "casting calls in" and your city or State. One such website for the Washington DC area is dragonukconnects.com.

Do you spend your free time doing something really unique like trying to bypass the security of computer programs? Yes, I'm talking about hacking. Companies like Facebook will pay you for discovering bugs in their software that could lead to their being hacked. According to Computer World, 13 August 2013, Google pays $1000 - $5000 for each significant bug found in their Chrome browser. Of curse you have to be the first to tell them. You also can't "test" their software in a way where you actually hack or embarrass them.

Don't forget contests!

If you are passionate about activities such as running, bicycling, weight lifting, wrestling, cooking, and art, are there contests in your area that have prizes? Cash prizes are handed out for more than just bikini contests. Though I have met women who make a lot of money on the side as regulars in the area's bikini contests.

Raid your closet of unwanted stuff!

One basic way to make extra money is to sell stuff. Empty out the attic, closets, basement and garage. What have you not touched for four years? A lot of it may have some cash value. There are lots of avenues open to you. Does your work have a bulletin board in the break room or have a website to sell stuff? At the worst, you can donate the items to Goodwill and claim it as a tax deduction.

Yard sales
Flea markets
Amazon.com is for more than old books.
CraigsList.com
Ebay.com

If you get good at selling you can make a hobby by going to yard sales and flea markets, hunting for under priced stuff you can resale at a profit!

Make Money as an Author

When I first started writing I knew a married couple who were professional writers. The main piece of advice they gave me was to write as a hobby and if one day I made more at that than my day job, then and only then, consider doing it for a living. It's not bad advice.

There are a lot of ways to make money as an author. You can get a journalism degree and work for a news outlet. Or, if you have a technical background, you can do technical writing. Both are hard to do part time unless you are already in the field. But if you like to write there are ways of making some extra money on the side.

Many people dream of writing a novel. So why not? It can be a great adventure. Expect to spend about 500 hours. A short story can be an easier project but you need as many as a dozen for a book. Or you can write an article for a magazine. One or two pages long is a good size for an article.

Earlier in this book I told the story of the boat owner who taught sailing classes on the side. The idea of writing your own textbook and making your students buy it is a common practice at major Universities. Professors are more likely to do this to satisfy the "print or perish" clause in their contracts than to make a profit. They then put out a new version every year or two for the same reasons. Making your students use your own text book ensures there is a market, giving the publisher confidence that they can turn at least a modest profit. Because the guaranteed number of sales is relatively low, the text books have to be very expensive for the venture to work out.

Selling an article or short story the old fashioned way

Let's say you write one article on something you know and one short story. Go to a book store and look at all of the magazines on the same subject as your article or magazines that contain stories on the same subject as your piece. On the front page, maybe the second is the publisher's contact information. It could be a website. Or it could be a old fashioned mailing address. The editor is who you want to send your article or story to. Include a cover letter with a one or two paragraph summary of your piece. Also have a copy on a CD. You'll want to include and SASE (self addressed stamped envelop) for your work to be mailed back to you if they don't like it. If they respond with a rejection, it can take as much as three months for you to receive it. Frequently you will never hear back. So, after three to four months, send your piece off to the next editor.

Submit to one magazine or anthology at a time. Never send to multiple at the same time. This will cause trouble if suddenly two send you a contract to sign.

Unfortunately, this is the 21st Century and there aren't very many traditional publishers left. Still, the old fashioned way might work and worth a try. It's how you get a paycheck up. This is how I started. I was a clueless engineering student and my computer article sold. I was paid $80 for one page. That was back in 1982. My next one sold for $300. With repeated sales to the same publisher, they will pay you at a higher scale. The most I was ever paid was $1300.

What was my secret? I was in the right place at the right time. I had stumbled onto a hot market. I was published twenty four times before the market dried up. I wasn't published again for some time. That didn't mean that I stopped writing as a hobby.

Selling an article or a short story the new fashioned way

It's a new century and e-publishing is where the action is. That doesn't mean it is easy sailing. It is just that the rules of the game have changed. With traditional publishing it takes a long time to find out if you have made a sale. Then you get a contract followed by a check. Maybe you get royalties later on, if there are reprints.

With e-publishing it is easy to get published but you have to do all of the work. You also have to do the marketing. If you sell 100 copies, which is good for most ebooks, this equates to getting paid 20 cents an hour or less. Not good if you need to pay the bills. It's an OK start if you are merely trying to use your hobby to make some beer money.

The up side is that if you are in the right place at the right time, you could sell a million copies. The profits would buy you a new car and home.

Beware of companies that ask for a fee to help you get published. You can do this for free. You can get a professional image for your book cover for $5. You need a copy of Microsoft Word and an image editing tool that can save Jpeg's at 300 dpi wouldn't hurt. There are free ones on the internet.

For a road map that'll get you through the process from proof reading to advertising, check out my book, The Independent Author's Handbook - Second Edition. It is available in all ebook formats, Kindle and paperback.

Videos:

Writing your Novel While on the Go
Creating your Ebook Book Cover
Add Hyperlinks to your E-book
YouTube Video Advertisements

Beyond e-books

There is an excitement to be able to say you have written a book. You can point to a page on Amazon or iTunes and see your work. It's exciting to see your name in print. To have a professionally printed paperback in your hand is even better. Beware of websites that charge you for the pleasure of having a printed copy. I highly recommend the print on demand company, CreateSpace.com. They are free. They only charge you a percentage on each sale. I talk about them in detail in my author's book.

To be an author is to write and be read. There are many forms of writing. One is a blog. Nobody goes, "Wow! I can't believe you have a blog!" But you can reach an audience faster and easier than with e-books. The structure of a blog is a large number of short articles. You can either have a focused theme or a fairly random series of subjects. Either way, you need dozens of ideas. When in doubt, people love lists. You can do product reviews, clever little tales or become the answer guy.

No matter what website you have your blog on, be sure to fill out the tag/label/keyword section for each of your articles. This is key for people to find you through Google and Bing.

If you see typos after your article has been published, be sure to fix them. Unlike the printed word, you can easily tweak, fix and expand your blog articles anytime you like.

How you make money is from ad revenue. You need to pick a blog website that will let you decide whether there will be ads next to your articles or not. Many won't. The ones that do will give you a piece of the action if you say yes. Blogspot.com will. To create an account and post articles, you have to go to Blogger.com. They are displayed on the "BlogSpot" website.

But where to start? You need an Adsense account. This is who selects, posts and manages your advertisements. Start this whole adventure out by surfing to Adsense.com and create an account. When it asks if you want a free blog (blogspot), say yes!

Adsense will manage everything and at the end of each month, wire money into your bank account assuming they owe you $100 or more. This won't happen when you start out. But as you post more and more articles, it will come to pass eventually. What you get paid is based on a complex and daily changing schedule. It averages out to about one cent per one hundred hits in your articles. You get between a couple of cents to a dollar is somebody clicks on an ad. But don't go clicking on the ads yourself. They'll spot it and ban you from their websites.

I received nothing per month in the beginning. Then it was five cents one month. Then sixteen cents. I wrote five articles a month and in eight months, I was making $26 a month. This was for a readership of 20,000 a month. But how much money an hour does this equate to? Let's assume you have written 130 articles, taking 100 hours to write. Assuming the ad income is $10 a month which goes on for four years, this comes to about $3.6 per hour. If your articles are more interesting than mine, you might make significantly more money. It only takes one going viral to really up your paycheck.

Beware of posting copyrighted material. There are law firms that are dedicated to suing websites that don't have permission for their content. You can lose your house over this. However, you can link to other people's web content as long as it is obvious you are not taking credit for their work. If you are writing an article about road construction, it is reasonable to imbed You Tube videos that demonstrate the use of the various machines you describe.

To Write is to be Pirated

It is a backhanded kind of complement isn't it. Especially if you struggle to get published or sell copies. It is tempting to do nothing but complain. Still, it is your intellectual property and you need to protect it. Every situation is different. To date I've stopped pirates in their tracks four times.

I discovered one weekend that I had once again been pirated. A copy of my cookbook was for sale on Amazon (Kindle) under a different title but retaining my name. How did I discover it? I had just published a new collection of time travel stories (Wasn't Tomorrow Wonderful) and had gone to Author Central to add it to my Kindle's author's page. It sometimes is a challenge to find your new book. I searched for the title then I searched for my name. After several screens of book covers, my cookbook appeared. I had never published it on Amazon so it immediately caught my eye.

How do you report a problem like this to Amazon? Good question. Amazon like Google makes it hard to send a human an email. Surprisingly, they also make it hard to alert them about copyright infringement since they are working very hard behind the scenes to thwart this very problem.

Report pirated copies of your book being sold on Amazon by sending an email to **copyright@Amazon.com**. You need to state that you are the real author and the problem is copyright infringement. Give them the title your work is published under and **ASIN number**. You can get this off the webpage selling the pirated book. It's just over half way down the web page.

   - Your address, telephone number

   - A statement by you that you have a good-faith belief that the disputed use is not authorized by the copyright owner, its agent, or the law.

   - ASIN number. The URL of the webpage may work if you are having trouble spotting the ASIN.

   Expect an email from Amazon asking you to confirm the violation. It will be several days before the book is removed.

   If the problem is not a straightforward copyright violation, you can contact a system administrator. From your Kindle Author Central page. At the very bottom, in the center in small letters is "Contact us". Click on it. For the "The subject" choose "My Books" and the "Details" would be set to "Other". Lastly, select "E-mail" and briefly describe the problem.

   If you want more examples of how pirates steal from you and several ideas how to stop them, you might like my book, **The Independent Author's Handbook - Second Edition**. It is available in paperback, Kindle and all other e-book formats

Make Money by making Movies!

Do you make movies or videos as a hobby? Ever try to make a few dollars off of it? There are a couple of ways you may not have thought of.

The place to post your videos is You Tube! Maybe you have already done this. If you haven't, it's not hard. All you need is a hundred dollar digital camera and a twenty dollar tripod. Please use a tripod! To edit your videos, you can use Windows Moviemaker Live that comes free with your computer if the operating system is Microsoft Windows. If you want to use a sound track, best to add it after you upload to You Tube. It is the Audio option when you edit your uploaded video. Otherwise, you risk the You Tube bots accusing you of using copyrighted music.

If you decide to use a music track and also decide to use You Tube's library, be sure your video is no longer than three minutes. Why? Because, the average length of a song is about three minutes. There are very few ten minute long songs and instrumentals. Odds are, it won't match the theme for your video. And having music for the first half of your work and silence for the second half just won't be satisfying. Thus do yourself and your attention challenged audience a favor and try not to make any videos that are over three minutes.

A You Tube account is free. Once you have your first video uploaded, you can open an Adsense account. Adsence.com is the website that selects, posts and manages the ads on your videos. Now go back to You Tube and "monetize" your account.

To monetize your account, go to Settings. At the bottom, click on "View additional features". On the left will be the word, "monetize". Click on it and follow the steps. For some reason, the initial setup to post ads on your videos has always been an awkward process. The result is that the steps you have to follow to accomplish this changes from time to time.

Adsense will wire into your bank account money at the end of each month assuming they owe you $100 or more. This won't happen when you start out. But as you post more and more videos, it will come to pass eventually. What you get paid is based on a complex and daily changing schedule. It works out to about one cent per one hundred hits in your videos. You get between a several cents to a dollar is somebody clicks on an ad. But don't go clicking on the ads yourself. They'll spot it and ban you from their websites.

Your goal is to create a lot of short videos. Short videos are more popular than long ones. Try to keep yours to less than three minutes. Keep the subject in the upper two thirds of the screen. The overlaid ads will cover the lower third. If the viewer can see your video without having to close the ad, they may let it run. You get paid more the longer the ad is being viewed.

Once your videos are uploaded, you need to give them a title and description. A list of tags is critical. These are keyword related to your video. How most people will find you by doing searches on subjects that interest them.

Go to your video manager then edit your video a second time. You'll see a monetization tab. Go into it and turn on the ads for your video. I have found that the "TrueView in-stream ads" (TV ads) chase off viewers. Only use these when you can a video people really want to see. Otherwise stick to the Overlay in-video ads.

It is hard to predict what videos will be popular. Try a variety of subjects. You may stumble into one that really brings in an audience. Some people write skits or perform stand up comedy. I have more of a reporter angle to mine. Whenever I have a topic or experience that I think somebody might find interesting, I try to express it in a couple of paragraphs. When I film, I change the camera angle every couple of sentences. The frequent camera movement helps keep the viewer's interest and I have less to memorize. If I screw up a line, I don't have to redo the whole video over. I can keep filming the same brief moment over and over until it is acceptable. Editing is much easier if you have lots of short clips rather than one big one.

I have several running themes. They are: Amusing and Unexpected, Slight of Hand (magic tricks), Dealing with Natural Disasters, Art and Photography, Ways to Save a Dollar, Bike Trails (test drive them), Review of Cool Gadgets, Family Cookbook, Science Projects and Travel Advice.

Some of your videos will be much better than others. That is to be expected. Over time you'll become more comfortable with talking on film. It is unpredictable what subject or which video in a string of the same subject will bring in the viewers so keep trying. All you need is one to go viral to start bringing in the money.

Do date I have about 192 videos averaging three minutes long and have 140,000 viewers a month across this body of work. It takes me about two hours to make a video. Based on my monthly ad revenue and the assumption I'll keep my viewer ship for about four years, making videos pays me $29 per hour. You likely won't see this yourself with just one video. It might only get 15 hits in its lifetime or you might get 400 hits a day. Most likely you will have to make quite a few before they average out to a number like this.

If you have both a blog and make videos, look for subjects that can do double duty. I have found that many of the people who read blogs don"t view a lot of videos. So, if you can express yourself on a subject in a video and then again in written words, you will tap two different audiences. If you can imbed your video in your blog article, you may even be able to get double ad credit per hit.

The biggest downside to You Tube are the Haters. The impersonal aspect of the internet allows people to act differently than they would if they were standing in front of you. The worst of them are the "Haters". They are people, usually male teenagers with anger issues. You Tube is Hater central.

Each video has a dedicated blog under it. People will comment on your video and chat back and forth to each other. Some people will insult other viewers because screwing with strangers can be fun. The Haters will throw temper tantrums, usually at you. In general ignore them all. There is nothing to gain by confronting Haters. They have emotional issues. You're not going to get them to apologize. The most you can do it delete their offensive blog entry.

People bickering at each other can be a benefit. A wrestling match on your video's blog means a lot of hits. Every time they go to your page to squabble with each other or make fun of your video, ka-ching! You get ad credit.

Income Taxes

If you are receiving ad revenue from a blog or videos, it will be reported to the IRS as income. This is not a problem when you start out and only receive pennies a month. Once you achieve a couple hundred dollars a month, this comes to a couple thousand a year. Depending on your tax bracket, you may be paying as much as a third of this in taxes at the end of the year.

But wait! This is a business model. You are writing articles or making videos to make a profit. Thus you can deduct business expenses on your taxes. If you make videos and bought a camera and tripod, it is a deduction. If you do a product review keep a receipt of what you bought. If you do a review of that whale watching trip, how much did it cost? Don't forget the car rental for the day and gas to get there. The key is not to claim more in expenses than what you made for the entire year. Showing a consistent loss on your taxes for year after year will only beg the IRS to audit you.

Make extra money by providing a service

Providing a service is based on what you know or what you have. For example, if you have a pickup truck you can haul things for a fee. You can haul large awkward trash or tree branches to the dump. If you are a roofer by trade, you can moonlight doing roof repair.

The advantage of the following list of ideas is that you only have to work when you want to. You don't have to when you don't want to.

You only get one
first impression

Be sure to dress well. It may be fine to dress gangster with your friends or in dirty torn clothes around the house but to get strangers to hire you, you must be clean and professional looking. Clean your car. If the customers come to your home for any reason, keep both the inside and outside clean and neat in the areas they are likely to see. If you don't look like you have your act together, you won't get any work.

Make use of what you know

Know what you are doing. Don't learn on your clients. A disaster can be costly!

I had an in-ground pool with beautiful, randomly shaped black slate surrounding it. The grout between the slate was disintegrating. It looked

like a fairly big job. I didn't want to tackle it myself.
It just so happened that a friend of a neighbor was out
of work. I talked to him and he told me he knew how
to grout tiles. Not a problem! He needed some
money and I'd get the job done for half. It looked like
a win-win.

He assured me he knew what he was doing.
He really wanted to please me. He used the wrong
grout. Instead of latex based he used epoxy based.
He assured me it would last forever. It turned out that
he didn't know what he was doing. It was a mess!
He had bought the wrong color. It was rough to the
feet such as it would cut the feet of the children when
they walked around the pool! There were ghostly
epoxy hand prints everywhere. What a mess! Being
epoxy it wouldn't come back up! It was permanent.

You know the old saying, "No good deed goes
unpunished". The guy had wrecked my pool. I had
to bring in a company to repair the mess. The bill
was $12,000! In the end, I had them to tear it all up
and throw away the black slate. They put down a
fake slate like material. It cost me $6,000. I could
have killed him. If he wasn't in the process of losing
his house I would have sued him.

**If you don't know what you are doing,
do not fake it.
You'll only regret it.**

But what if you don't have any skills? There
is a way to practice on other people's houses without
getting into trouble. Check with your family,
neighbors or workmates. Somebody always has a

project going on. You can volunteer to be an extra pair of hands. For receiving the payment price of pizza and beer, you can get hands on experience. Hopefully, they know what they are doing. If they don't, you might get a valuable lesson is what not to do.

When I was in my 20's I was on a strict budget for the first few years. I watched my spending so closely that a few free meals here or there helped me get through those lean times. Later, the skills I learned this way help me by not having to hire a handyman every time I had a job to do.

Return of the part-time servants

There is a big market for somebody who is handy around the house. Even if they have the skills themselves, most people are very busy and need a little help once in a while. In the US we have an aging population. The elderly, handicapped and shut-ins need a level of assistance beyond average people. In Victorian times and before, servants were the norm. What is forgotten is that most servants were specialized and part time. Often, servants had their own part time servants. How do you do your laundry when you have to work all of the time?

A handyman or rent-a-husband, as one business has coined it can be a source of endless extra income. You can advertise by posting flyers next to the community mailboxes that many houses in developments have now a days.

Don't post on a US Mail postal box. Many grocery stores, public libraries and some employers have a bulletin board you can post a flyer. You can put flyers under car windshield wipers if they are in a parking lot. Online there are websites such as Craig's list. Be sure to list the types of jobs you are interested in doing. Some may be too big but no job is too small for a handyman! Here is a list to help you brainstorm.

Indoors:

Caulk a tub or window.
Paint a room.
Install or replace light fixtures, chandelier or flood lights.
Install or replace a ceiling or attic fan.
Put up sheet rock.
Install carpeting.
Install modular shelves in a closet.
Replace appliances such as a garbage disposal.
Help people move. Using your own truck is good but not necessary.

Do you have a carpet cleaner? There are chemicals, bottles to fill, hoses and attachments. This can be a great one to specialize over. Just the act of driving to the store to rent one then return it afterwards is daunting to many people. If you own a carpet cleaner you are in great shape as you likely know how to use it properly. About all you need to determine is how many square feet a bottle of your favorite carpet cleaner and deodorizer will do. Tip. Be sure that the carpet is in good shape. Refuse the job if the carpet looks dubious. I once had a heavily worn carpet disintegrate on me. You don't want an angry customer demanding you re-carpet their room.

Outside your home:

Replace rotted molding around a door or window.

Replace a flood light.

Replace lost shingles.

Pressure wash vinyl sided houses and decks. Beware of damaging wood. Pressure washers will take the paint off of wood and aluminum siding.

Repairing or resealing an asphalt driveway can be a good one to specialize on. This is a messy but not very time consuming job. The typical driveway can be sealed with one to two tubs of sealer. If you need two tubs and work for 90 minutes, you charge $100 for the job. After spending $60 on the sealer you would make over $26 an hour.

Teenagers don't do
yard work anymore

Mow a lawn. Most teenagers don't do odd jobs any more. There is still a need to have lawns mowed when people go on vacation in the summer. Unmarried business travelers need this done as often as once a week when they are on the road.

Repair a fence.

Build or repair a retention wall.

Replace the rusted out burner in a gas grill.

Replace the wood on a deck.

Build a deck.

Trim bushes.

Trim trees. You can rent a chainsaw at a rent-a-center but will need a truck to haul away the branches.

Wash and vacuum out cars.

Haul trash to the local dump.

Shovel snow. In the winter, driveways and sidewalks need to get shoveled. If you have a gas powered snow blower, you can really clean up! (Pun intended) When I was ten, I made $100 a house by shoveling roofs.

As an adult, it snowed two feet in one storm. I had thrown my back out and unable to shovel. I desperately needed but was unable to find anybody to shovel it for me. I would have paid very well. Now think about all of the elderly and people with heart conditions. In most neighborhoods there is a potentially large market for a person with a snow blower.

Don't be afraid to specialize. With energy costs high, you can learn to tint windows. I've done it to two houses now and have seen my summer cooling cost drop in half. If you want to know more about this, check out my You Tube of did about it, Easy Tint for your Home.

There is never a pool boy around when you need one!

I used to travel for work. Having a swimming pool, I needed somebody to take care of it. There were no businesses in my area with pool boys. I was willing to pay triple minimal wage and provide the training. No takers! All they had to do was show up once a week, vacuum and if needed, dump a measured amount of chemicals in the water. If it got out of control, they were to take a water sample to the pool store and do whatever they said. I would reimburse for any chemicals needed. For that matter, I could have made arrangements with the pool company to charge me directly. It was a guaranteed $40 a week for a half hour's work. I never found a taker.

If there are homes in your area with pools, it can be worth your while to pursue this. Odds are several will want somebody they can call at only once in a while. Most pool owners not only will train you but will insist on showing you how they check and clean the pool and filter. They may even will pay you for you time while they are training you.

A must have is a car. You need to be able to run to the pool store and haul back twenty pounds of chemicals.

Beyond vacuuming and cleaning the filter, learning to open and close pools is a very welcome service.

Rent a Wife

At the risk of sounding sexist, there are plenty of opportunities for a "rent a wife" type services.

Baby sitting is a great one for a housewife or other able but home centric people. Many couples and single parents need a place with supervision for their child or children to stay until they get off of work. Most states will let you take care of up to three children before requiring a license.

Many couples and single parents desperately need a date night once in a while. If they can drop off their child before dinner and pick them up at two in the morning, you'll get more work than you can handle! You can also charge double or triple minimal wage without people blinking an eye. That is for just one child!

If you have an in-demand language skill, you might be able to charge a premium. Besides watching and feeding the child, you can teach them a second language.

Outside the US, American English is popular. Teaching a second language can be sought after by people of any age. You can teach English to support a young person passing a college entrance exam. You'll want to have both an instruction guide and a study guide. Have the student watch popular TV shows and news broadcasts such as CNN and write about it to prove they understood the content. You may need to have to be TOEF certified. To learn more about this go to ets.org.

If you are a non-native speaker, you can tutor that. There are plenty of language students who need a native speaker to help them hone their skills.

Children aren't the only ones that need occasional sitting. If you are a nurse, you can watch the elderly. You need to check your local laws to know if you need a license for this. In most cases this is not needed. But since the elderly are more likely to need medical care or have a medical emergency, you might get in over your head if you don't have some medical training. It could be as simple as learning CPR.

There is also a big market for dog walking and pet sitting. One specialized website to advertise baby sitting of children and pets is care.com.

If you are already caring for a handicapped sibling or elderly parent, you might be able to get paid for it. If this person is on Medicaid, you'll want to get on the "Medicaid Waiver List". There would be an evaluation of the health care need. But successfully being accepted by the Living at Home Waiver Program, means you can be hired by your sibling or parent as the in-home health care provider.
The concept is that it is less expensive for the patient to be cared for at home than in a hospital or institution. If the care is primarily cooking meals, helping get to the bathroom, in and out of bed, up and down the stairs, the patient is able to hire a family member, paying for the labor using Medicaid funds. This program is run by each individual State and there may be a limited number of people who can be accepted per year.
If you are in Georgia, this online document is a good place to start. (unlockthewaitinglists.com/MedicaidWaiverManual.pdf)
If you are in Maryland, the waiver request form is 2009-06-03 201915_HCBS_Waiver_Maryland_0353_R02.

Bartender. You can get trained to be a bartender in four weeks. A gig at a wedding can make for an easy start as weddings usually provide their guests a very limited drink selection. Starting out in a bar, expect to be given the slow times, meaning the tips will be light. As you improve your skills and show your value, you'll be given more profitable work hours.

Here is a website that lists the minimal age to be a bartender. www.bartending.org/bartending-ages.html. Surprisingly, in many states an 18 year old can bartend.

Cooking meals (especially if you are a chef). Elderly and handicapped people need occasional help in all sorts of unexpected ways. Some people just don't know how to cook. If you do, you could cook several meals and put them into single serving containers in the client's refrigerator or freezer. You could cook at their house or your own and deliver meals once a week. This could easily expand into helping people cook for parties. From here it is an easy leap into full time catering.

Grocery shopping service. Charge for your time plus 50 cents per mile.
Ironing.
Laundry.
Wash windows.
Vacuuming.

Proof reading. Everybody is an author these days. The market for proofreading manuscripts is larger than you might suspect. But you need to be a good speller and able to spot grammatical mistakes. Two places to advertise are on elance.com and Craig's List.

Typing. The minimum speed for a receptionist may be 35 words per minute and a secretary is in the neighborhood of 72. Many of the occasional part-time jobs lie in typing up a doctor's notes, perhaps written in short hand. An author might have a printed manuscript that needs to be typed into a word processor. If you are being paid for a task rather than by the hour, the faster you can accurately type, the sooner you get the task done, increasing your profit.

Ride sharing to work. You can just as easily do all of the driving and have the passengers pay the expenses. Maybe a little more. But beware of becoming an unofficial taxi. A license is required in most places. The existing taxi drivers may get very angry and aggressive exposing you to a different kind of hazard.

What to charge

If you are not somebody's employee, determining what to charge is always awkward. And you don't want to get greedy. There is a simple rule of thumb. Charge your time plus materials. How much for your time? It depends on how long the job takes. Charge for a minimal of one hour. If it's all day, how much do you make in your current job? At ten dollars an hour, that would be eighty dollars per day. This is reasonable, maybe inexpensive. One hundred dollars for eight hours ($12.50 per hour) may be reasonable to ask as long as it is noticeably less than what a business in the yellow pages would charge.

Big jobs like replacing a deck have a high material cost and take a couple of days to complete. It is reasonable to ask for half of the money up front. An alternative could be to get the material cost up front and get paid for the labor daily. But if you are charging by the hour and not the job, be careful not to give the impression that you are dragging it out.

Since you don't have management to take a cut and a store front to pay for, you may be able to charge much more and still be seen as very affordable. This overhead can be expensive to the customer. I know a business owner who charges his customers fifty dollars an hour. He is the cheapest company on the block. The actual workers who then do the job only get paid twelve dollars an hour. So in a situation like this, if you have the skills, you could charge thirty dollars an hour and everybody is happy.

To finish the story of the business owner, I had first thought he kept most of the money out of greed. Then I realized he was paying himself for more than just managing the day to day tasks and lining up future work. The money went to more than just himself.

Customers frequently don't pay their bills on time. The small business owner regularly has to take out short term high interest loans to cover payroll. As much as twenty percent of the customers have to be hounded for a long time before they pay. Many never pay. The small business owner may have to regularly risk losing their home to cover payroll. The business owner gets paid last if there is any money left over. With every customer, the small business owner may have to swallow the cost of the job. This is where much of that fifty dollars an hour goes. But the customer doesn't see this. All they see is that you'll charge them half or less for the same job.

Do you need a license?

When you are a child, you can do a chore, sell lemonade and throw a yard sale with no thought to taxes and legal restrictions. Once you become an adult this unfortunately changes. Unless you are intentionally starting a business, this is a subject you may not give a second thought. You are doing odd jobs here and there. You're not a business. You aren't building new homes. You don't have a storefront. You're doing tasks that are too small and infrequent for a real business to care about. You're just helping other people out. At the most you are their temporary employee.

This thinking is not always correct. To do handyman jobs and be a part time servant you might actually need a license or a certification. This line between what requires a license and what doesn't is different in every State. All try to define the line by listing specific jobs. Some States also use a minimum dollar amount. If you charge the customer for the odd job below a certain amount you don't need a contractor's license. Above this magical line and you do. This can be anywhere from $500 to $3000 and is subject to change. It is a "Minor Work Exemption" rule. In California it is currently $500.

**In Wisconsin,
you need a license to give a massage
but not to repair a car engine.**

A common theme is repairing and cleaning doesn't require a license. Improving a property does. Without the proper licenses, you can't advertise. Meaning you cannot run TV ads or represent yourself as a business. How you would find customers should be kept small scale and low key. The "Air B and B" story was an example of having too high a profile and while lacking the proper licenses.

In a situation where you might get hurt, like working on a roof or might cause serious damage or the customer may demand the job redone by a very expensive professional you need liability insurance. As a guideline on this subject, a general contractor's license requires having a minimal of $50,000 of liability insurance.

Disability insurance would be prudent. If you fall of a roof, suing your customer isn't a great option. Insurance should be your first safety net.

What often doesn't need a license:

Assembling a shed on a non permanent foundation such as dirt or cinder blocks.

Chimney sweeps; cleaning chimneys. Chimney repairs may require a license.

Clean residences of dirt or debris.

Clean carpet.

Demolition and clean-up work.

Installing carpet is not within the definition of "home improvement".

Installing wall-mounted televisions or home theatres in residences.

Installing curtain hooks, rods and hanging curtains and drapes may or may not require a license depending the State, County and city.

Plugging a hot tub into a 220V outlet with a marine cover. But wiring a hot tub to a circuit breaker would require a license.

Where a license is needed:

Some handyman jobs need a license. Some don't. To obtain a general contractor's license, a person must have at least four years of qualified experience. You will have to show proof that you have experience working as a journeyman, specializing in a specific field such as carpentry or plumbing. The following are examples of type of the work that in most States would require a license.

Install tile, wood, or other flooring is considered a home improvement.

Install a central vacuum system in a residence is a home improvement because the installation is permanently affixed to the house or property.

Building or reinforcing the chimney, or installing a chimney cap,

Painting the interior or exterior of a house.

This includes decorative painting.

Adding or extending a driveway, including gravel driveways.

Installing patios and retaining walls at a residence.

Trimming, pruning, thinning, cabling, shaping, removing, or reducing the crown of a tree that is 20 feet or taller.

Building a swing set or jungle gym at residence home, if it is sunk into the ground.

Electrical and plumbing.

Food preparation always needs some level of licensing, certificates and inspections. If you go into somebody's home and cook a meal in the customer's kitchen with their food, you are classified as a "personal chef" and need a Food and Safety Certificate, a food handler's license and a personal chef's license (DBA) or a business license. Depending on your State, you may also need a catering license. Catering is often defined as simple as "providing food preparation services". The American Personal and Private Chef Association and the American Culinary Federation provide certification training for personal chefs. Contact your local state and county licensing department to find out what licenses are required for private chefs in your area.

Although you don't need to be a trained cook to be a personal chef, acquiring the needed legal documents may be more effort and cost than you want to deal with for a part time job. If you already are a line cook or chef you would have most of the legal requirements satisfied. The extra step of obtaining a business license wouldn't be a significant hurdle.

A personal chef cannot deliver prepared food. Preparing food in your home would minimally require a catering license, permit and inspection followed by an approval from the department of health. Expect requirements such as there cannot be a pet in your home and the kitchen must not be a public space. This means it is behind a closed door that can be locked, keeping the other occupants and visitors out.

Income Taxes:

According to the IRS's website, there is no minimum amount of income that doesn't have to be reported.

"Fees received for babysitting, housecleaning and lawn cutting are all examples of taxable income, even if each client paid less than $600 for the year. Someone who repairs computers in his or her spare time needs to report all monies earned as self-employment income even if no one person paid more than $600 for repairs."

"Bartering is an exchange of property or services. The fair market value of goods and services exchanged is fully taxable and must be included on Form 1040 in the income of both parties."

"An example of bartering is a plumber doing repair work for a dentist in exchange for dental services."

About the Author

John Stilwell was born and raised in the Midwest. In the 1980's he was regularly published in popular computer magazines. He was a contributing author to three Commodore Computer books. He earned two degrees in Electrical Engineering. Today, he is an Engineer by day and an author and artist by night.

He has traveled extensively overseas with his hobbies being various and regularly changing. They have ranged from studying massage to bungee jumping. In the 1990's he learned to draw and produced a respectable quantity, selling an occasional piece.

In the late 2000's his daughter talked him into doing science projects together and creating youtube videos. Some include a leaf blower powered one-man hovercraft, a solar powered hot air balloon cam and various magnetic levitation curiosities.

By 2010 he was back into serious writing, focusing on books and articles.

Appendix A: Useful links

Acting:

Google "casting calls in" and your city or State. dragonukconnects.com sends out casting calls to the DC area.

Advertise your services:

Care.com for baby sitting, adult care and pets walking and sitting.
Elance.com
CraigsList.com

Advertise a room or house for rent:

ApartmentGuide.com
CraigsList.org
EasyRoommate.com
ForRent.com
Rent.com
RoommateLocator.com
Vrbo.com
Zillow.com

Background checks and credit scores:

Three credit bureaus are Experian, TransUnion, and Equifax.

Google the key words "sex offender registry" adding the State of interest.

Google the search term, "Judiciary Case Search" including the State of interest.

Reverse number lookup at WhitePages.com

Area code lookup at WhitePages.com

Bartending:

Minimal age to be a bartender www.bartending.org/bartending-ages.html.

Certification to teach a language:

Ets.org to learn more about getting an TOEF certification.

Collecting money:

PayPal.com

iPhone and an account. The "Square Credit Card Reader" is MacMall Part number: 972087, Manufacturer Part number: R01A1W.

House hunting:

Redfin.com to find houses for sale in the area you are interested in.

Zillow.com to see how much a house and its neighbors are worth. You also get the historical curve. If the house has an addition, or major upgrade, Zillow might not know about it.

AreaVibes.com provides stats about the neighborhood, the local population's local income, nearby amenities, and rates the local schools. The crime stats can give you an accurate feeling an area is worse than really is. Recommend you enter your current address first to get a sense of what the stats really mean.

CrimeReports.com shows you a map with icons representing where crimes of various times have occurred. It also shows where the sex offenders live along with a picture of their face. This site's data is comprehensive for some cities and lacking in others.

Legal Papers and Licenses:

AllPropertyManagement.com/propertylaw/

LegalZoom.com is a good source for contract.

Maryland Department of labor, licensing and regulations, FAQ's

USDA's National Organic Program webpage

Medicaid:

Georgia: MedicaidWaiverManual.pdf

Maryland: 2009-06-03%201915_HCBS_Waiver_Maryland_0353_R02.pdf

Publishing:

Adsense.com to manage advertising on your blog, videos and website.

BigStockPhoto.com to sell digital images and photos.

Write your blog on Blogger.com. Your blog articles will appear on Blogspot.com.

CreateSpace.com for paperbacks and CD's.

KDP.amazon.com for Kindle.

Smashwords.com for all other e-book formats. Will get you into iTunes, Sony, Barnes and Noble and more.

YouTube.com for videos.

Pirated on Amazon.com? Sent an email to copyright@Amazon.com

Stocks:

Carlson's book, "No Load Stocks"

Google "no-load stock." One site is noload.info.